THIS JOURNAL BELONGS TO

_____

Cover Design: Megan Werner
Cover Illustration: solodkayamari / stock.adobe.com
Layout & Design: Megan Werner

For permission requests, please contact the publisher at:
Mango Publishing Group
2850 S Douglas Road, 4th Floor
Coral Gables, FL 33134 USA
info@mango.bz

For special orders, quantity sales, course adoptions and corporate sales, please email the publisher at sales@mango.bz. For trade and wholesale sales, please contact Ingram Publisher Services at: customer.service@ingramcontent.com or +1.800.509.4887.

The Bird Lover's Blank Journal

ISBN: (print) 978-1-64250-950-2
BISAC category code: SEL045000, SELF-HELP / Journaling

yellow pear ◖ press

CPSIA information can be obtained
at www.ICGtesting.com
Printed in the USA
JSHW020156160422
25004JS00004B/8